Ruckus in the Garden

a comedy by
David Farr

Resource Material by
Suzy Graham-Adriani
and
Anthony Banks

William Collins' dream of knowledge for all began with the publication of his first book in 1819. A self-educated mill worker, he not only enriched millions of lives, but also founded a flourishing publishing house. Today, staying true to this spirit, Collins books are packed with inspiration, innovation and a practical expertise. They place you at the centre of a world of possibility and give you exactly what you need to explore it.

Collins. Do more.

Published by Collins
An imprint of HarperCollins*Publishers*
77–85 Fulham Palace Road
Hammersmith
London
W6 8JB

Commissioned by Charlie Evans
Design by JPD
Cover design by Charlotte Wilkinson
Production by Simon Moore
Printed and bound by CPI Bath

Acknowledgements

Photo credits: Aquarius Collection, pp82, 85; DHA Lighting/Rosco, p.81; Heritage Image Partnership Picture Library, pp71, 90, 91.

Browse the complete Collins catalogue at www.collinseducation.com

© HarperCollins*Publishers* Limited 2007.

10 9 8 7 6 5 4 3 2 1

ISBN-13 978-0-00-725488-0

David Farr asserts his moral right to be identified as the author of this work.

All rights reserved. No part of this publication may be reproduced, stored in a retrieval system or transmitted in any form or by any means – electronic, mechanical, photocopying, recording or otherwise – without the prior written consent of the Publisher or a licence permitting restricted copying in the United Kingdom issued by the Copyright Licensing Agency Ltd;, 90 Tottenham Court Road, London W1T 4LP.

All rights whatsoever in this work, amateur or professional are strictly reserved. Applications for permission for any use whatsoever, including performance rights, must be made in advance, prior to such proposed use, to St John Donald, PFD, Drury House, 34–43 Russell St, London WC2B 5HA. No performance may be given unless a licence has first been obtained.

British Library Cataloguing in Publication Data

A Catalogue record for this publication is available from the British Library

Contents

PLAYSCRIPT

Author's note — 4

Characters — 5

Playscript of *Ruckus in the Garden* — 6

RESOURCES

Staging the play — 70

Themes in and around the play — 83

Further reading and resources — 96

The Writer

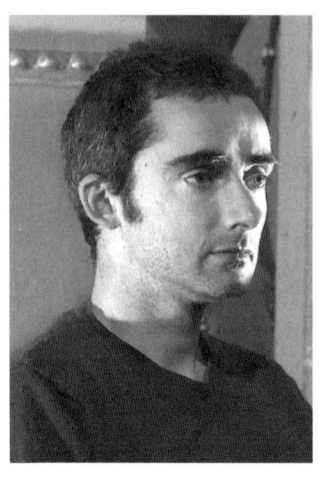

David Farr is a writer and director. He took up the post of Artistic Director of the Lyric Theatre Hammersmith in June 2005. He has just co-adapted and directed a highly successful production of Kafka's *Metamorphosis* for The Lyric with Icelandic actor/director Gisli Orn Gardarsson. His play *The UN Inspector*, a free adaptation of Gogol's *The Government Inspector*, opened at The National Theatre (Olivier) in June 2005 in his own production. His production of *Tamburlaine* played at The Barbican main stage in autumn 2005 to rave reviews. For The Lyric he has directed the Christmas show, *The Magic Carpet*, and *The Odyssey*.

David was Artistic Director of the Gate Theatre, London from 1995 to 1998, where his work earned him a reputation as one of the most exciting new talents in British theatre. He has subsequently been Joint Artistic Director of Bristol Old Vic from 2002 – 2005 with Simon Reade, turning the fortunes of the theatre around, directing seven shows including his versions of *Paradise Lost* and *The Odyssey* and winning the TMA Best Director Award for *A Midsummer Night's Dream*. He directed the award-winning *Coriolanus* (starring Greg Hicks) and *Julius Caesar* for the Royal Shakespeare Company, and has also worked for the Young Vic, Almeida Opera and the National Theatre of Czech Republic. As a playwright, David's work includes *The Nativity* at the Young Vic, *The Danny Crowe Show* at the Bush Theatre, *Elton John's Glasses* at Watford Palace and West End, *Crime and Punishment* in Dalston at the Arcola, and *Night of the Soul*, which he directed for the RSC at the Pit Theatre. He is published by Faber and Faber and writes regularly for the television series *Spooks*. His short comedy *The Queen Must Die* was part of NT Connections 2003.

Characters

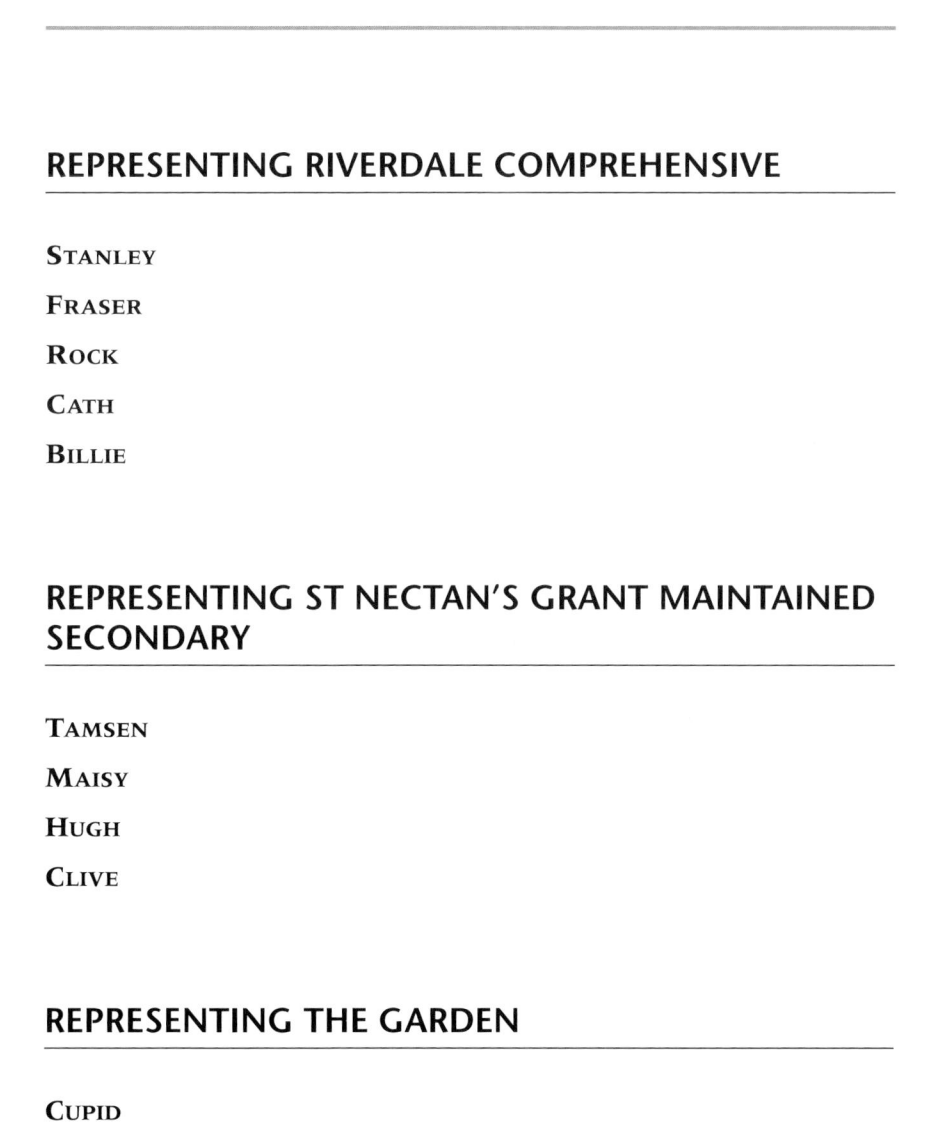

REPRESENTING RIVERDALE COMPREHENSIVE

STANLEY

FRASER

ROCK

CATH

BILLIE

REPRESENTING ST NECTAN'S GRANT MAINTAINED SECONDARY

TAMSEN

MAISY

HUGH

CLIVE

REPRESENTING THE GARDEN

CUPID

Ruckus in the Garden

Scene 1

The Garden of Cecil Fortescue. A warm late spring day. In the garden – **Stanley** *and* **Fraser**. *Both in their own clothes.*

FRASER	Where are we?
STANLEY	Read your Creative Partnerships Activity pack.
FRASER	Like I'm really going to do that.
STANLEY	Well if you did you would discover that we find ourselves at the entrance to Homesleigh – one of the great 18th century English landscape gardens.
FRASER	I'm going back to the coach.
STANLEY	*(reading)* Nestling in deep wooded countryside, Cecil Fortescue created Homesleigh in 1720 as a token of love for his French wife Amelia.
FRASER	Why didn't they take us to Alton Towers?
STANLEY	Stand at the entrance to the garden and look before you at the artificial lakes carved out of the landscape, Romanesque temples and statues dotted amidst abundant flora and shrubbery and the statues of Aphrodite, goddess of desire, and Apollo, god of unity and harmony.
FRASER	I can't stand all this fresh air. Makes me feel sick.
STANLEY	Look closer. A hundred small stone cupids dot

the landscape like guardian angels keeping watch over the sleeping greenery below. According to legend – when true lovers visit the garden the Cupids come alive and cause chaos and disarray with their mischievous arrows of desire. In this paradise of formal flowerbeds and sunken ha-has…

Fraser Sunken what?

Stanley Ha-ha. It's like a ditch.

Frazer If it's a ditch why don't they call it a ditch.

Stanley Put a sock in it … Cecil Fortescue…

Fraser Why do toffs have to invent new words for things that already have a name?

Stanley Cecil Fortescue brings Apollo and Aphrodite together to suggest that only through love and peace can the world achieve true harmony.

Fraser Last night I got so wasted I ended up puking in a ha-ha by the A36.

Beat. Enter **Rock**.

Rock You're not going to believe it. You know the other coach in the car park? The one with air con and head rests? It's only St Nectan's grant maintained.

Stanley Oh no.

Fraser OK, now we're talking.

Stanley Why does this happen every time?

Rock Stan? Is there going to be a ruckus?

Fraser You bet there is!

Rock	Between us and the St Nectan's boys?
Stanley	What do you think?
Rock	Jackson Miller says there is. Three pm in the temple of Apollo.
Frazer	Now this is a day out! We're gonna lick them bastards!
Rock	I don't like fights Stan.
Stanley	Nor do I Rock.
Rock	Yeah but you disapprove for moral and political reasons. I just get really scared.
Stanley	I disapprove because three hundred years after Cecil Fortescue made his garden of love and harmony we are still beating the crap out of the local selective secondary.
Fraser	We always fight St Nectan's on trips. It's cool.
Stanley	It's not cool. It's pathetic and degrading!
Fraser	We gonna whip their moneyed arses Stan man.
Stanley	And why? Because they've got purple blazers? Why Fraze?
Fraser	Cos they drive those new minis, and cos they have okra in their packed lunch. I dunno! Because we're on a school trip to a piss-boring garden and so are they, and they're grant maintained, and what else are we going to do? Smell the tulips?
Stanley	But it's all we ever do Fraze. Fix it so we go on school trips the same day as they do, have beefs with them, get caught, get grounded, do it again. I'm looking for a bit of evolution.

Rock	When we fought them at Whipsnade Zoo this big floppy haired guy called Moose broke Casey Martin's ankle.
Fraser	That's cos they're rugby players innit. But we got that sorted this time. We brought ammunition.
Rock	What ammunition?
Stanley	Read this Fraze. "It was the Greek vision of love and harmony that Cecil Fortescue set out to imitate – to create an idyll where love and peace would forever reign". The man was a revolutionary Fraser, and you're using his garden as a battleground!
Fraser	He was a posh git who wanted to bang his wife in a temple. They didn't have Golf GTIs in them days. He had to go with a quickie behind the statue of Venus.
Stanley	But don't you see Fraze that by fighting St Nectan's we are confirming every prejudice about Riverdale. We're chavs and sluts who can only express ourselves through the fist and they're a progressive academy who have been provoked into retaliation. It's just so depressing man.
Rock	Are you in a bad mood Stanley?
Fraser	He's just bitter cos he's been ha-ha'd by Kelly Fisher.
Stanley	I have not.
Fraser	Why were you seen weeping at the Megabowl?
Stanley	Kelly and I came to realise we had irreconcilable differences.
Fraser	You liked her, she didn't like you.

Rock	Don't be down Stan. She was wrong for you anyway.
Stanley	What do you mean?
Rock	I just don't think you were cut out for each other. You're an idealist. She was all cars and shoes and stuff.
Fraser	Having a good time. Laughing. Enjoying life. Shallow, shallow, shallow.
Stanley	You know we'll be blamed. It will be the same old story. The poor-unwashed-sink-school-scum attack the future of Britain. We always come off worse! If we are ever going to change our society – we have to make the first move.
Fraser	And how are we going to do that?
Stanley	I'll tell you how. I'm going to walk into this garden and the first St Nectan's boy I find – I'm going to shake his hand.
Fraser	Then the second thing you should do is duck.
Stanley	And then I'm going to invite that St Nectan's pupil to join with me in a peace, love and harmony action here in the garden.
Rock	That's suicide Stan. Don't do it.
Stanley	Someone has to. These fights are destroying us man. Asbos, exclusion orders… It's doing my head in.
Rock	What if you meet a girl?
Stanley	If it's a girl I'll kiss her on the cheek.

Beat.

Rock You won't…

Stanley The olive branch of reconciliation…

Rock She'll think you're trying to get off with her.

Stanley No she won't. She'll understand the nature of my approach and we'll walk in the garden hand in hand as Cecil Fortescue intended us to do.

Fraser If anyone from Riverdale sees you you'll get belted. And that includes me.

Stanley That's a price I'm prepared to pay Fraze.

Fraser OK but when you've made a right prize fool of yourself the ruckus is at three…

Stanley At the temple of Apollo. Yeah yeah.

Rock I'm gonna get whacked. I always get whacked.

Fraser Don't do this Stan.

Stanley I don't need no ruckus Frase. I'm going into the garden.

Scene 2

Cath and *Billie*, *also in their own clothes*

BILLIE	I want a cheeky fag. Maybe we can hide in the Arch of Artemis.
CATH	You saw.
BILLIE	Saw what?
CATH	When he got off the coach. I was right in front of him. He didn't even look at me.
BILLIE	He was being given his Creative partnerships activity pack by Mrs Gunnasekara.
CATH	He's been chucked by Kelly Fisher. He should be desperate for a sign of affection from even the most grievous minger. Walked right past me.
BILLIE	I don't see why you think he's so gorgeous anyway.
CATH	That's because you have absolutely no taste.
BILLIE	I have no taste? Look at your clothes Cath.

Beat.

CATH	What's wrong with my clothes?
BILLIE	Nothing.
CATH	He's always so sad. Like he's trying to reach out for something that isn't there.
BILLIE	Where's your activity pack?
CATH	I chucked it in the bin.
BILLIE	Cath! You'll get well in trouble for that.
CATH	What's the point? They only make them so they can get funding for the visit. Pick the worst school

	in the world and give them money to go to some "improving experience" like we'll all come out playing the violin and painting seascapes. Makes me sick man. *(grabs it)* "Spot the Obelisk". "Colour in the temple of Flora". Like what is that about?
BILLIE	What's wrong with you girl?
CATH	"Describe in thirty words how visiting the garden has changed your views on the nature of love". Like "hello"?
BILLIE	Cath? What's eating you?

Beat.

CATH	Am I a minger Bill?
BILLIE	No, of course not…
CATH	I wish I could change the way I looked. Wipe it all out and start again. I'd go online and buy Kelly Fisher's legs – click. Buy Bryony Sturrock's arse – click. Sandra Estevez's tits. Proceed to checkout.
BILLIE	Sandra Estevez has got the best tits in year ten.
CATH	Her dad's Brazilian.
BILLIE	Costa Rican.
CATH	Same difference.

Beat.

BILLIE	Are you gonna go to the ruckus?
CATH	Dunno.
BILLIE	Go on. Do you good to tear the face off some posh tart.
CATH	St Nectan's girls don't fight. They just sit on the wall giggling and swishing their pony tails.

BILLIE So we'll knock 'em off the wall. We've got ammo.

CATH Stanley doesn't believe in fighting.

BILLIE Oh for God's sake.

CATH He's a pacifist.

BILLIE That's one word for him.

CATH You know when you just get someone Bill. Like you know what ticks inside them without even talking to them. And the only obstacle is that they don't seem to be aware that you exist.

BILLIE Come on! Let's do the activity pack together. We can present it as a joint project – they love that kind of thing. And then we can get down to the grotto and help prepare the ambush.

CATH I do fancy smashing the daylights out someone.

BILLIE That's more like it!

CATH Go on then, what's the first question?

BILLIE They're not questions. They're challenges. Challenge One. Find ten trees and write down their Latin names.

CATH That is so exciting.

BILLIE And then we have to mark the location of thirty cupids on the map.

CATH You are kidding me.

BILLIE Listen girl. When did you last have a day out?

CATH Three years ago. My dad took us to Thorpe Park. I think it was by way of an early apology. Three days later he ran off with the hairdresser.

BILLIE So make the most of it. Come on!

Exeunt.

Scene 3

Inside the garden. **Tamsen** *and* **Maisy**. *In St Nectan's uniform.*

MAISY   How could they have let us come here on the same day as Riverdale! Riverdale should be doing something useful like visiting a remand centre or going on a hip-hop course.

TAMSEN   They don't scare me. I do tai kwan do.

MAISY   Now instead of being able to enjoy the neoclassical landscape, I'm going to spend all day hiding behind the shrubbery.

TAMSEN   I'm tougher than half those boys. I'll take them down.

MAISY   But didn't you get the text?

TAMSEN   What text?

MAISY   They don't want us fighting. They want the girls to be lookouts.

TAMSEN   Lookouts?

MAISY   We're meant to hide in the rhododendrons under the statue of cupid and make an owl-call if we see anything.

TAMSEN   That is sexist and patronising!

MAISY   Of course, what they didn't say is which cupid. There are cupids everywhere. I can't tell one from the other.

TAMSEN   I could bury my fist in one of those Riverdale boys any day!

MAISY The boys think you might be a bit of a loose cannon Tam.

TAMSEN What does that mean?

MAISY I think they're a bit scared of you. It's the way you only ever go out with any of them for a maximum of three days before ending it. They think you're unreliable.

TAMSEN You never go out with any of them either.

MAISY But I'm not asked. I'm seen as a stay-at-home-and-read-Jane-Austen type. You're tall and gorgeous but you're not interested in being their girlfriend.

TAMSEN Why should I be interested? And what if I am gorgeous? I'd love not to be. I'd love to blend into the crowd like you Mais. Then I wouldn't be treated like a trophy princess the whole bloody time!

MAISY It must be hard being that beautiful.

TAMSEN Damn right it is! And you know why I never go out with any of them for more than about a minute? Because they're not real men. They're loathsome, wannabee public schoolboys who have already planned their careers in law, what wife to marry, what Audi to buy, what coffin to be buried in. Where's the romance in that? Where's the passion? Part of me hopes they're blown to smithereens by Riverdale. They may be a bunch of chavs but at least they're in the moment.

MAISY What about Hugh Phillips? I thought you really liked him, but now you've ended that too.

TAMSEN Yeah well…

Maisy	I really thought he might be different…
Tamsen	Yeah well…
Maisy	He's sensitive, clever, and he's so good-looking.
Tamsen	Yeah all right Maisy! If he's so bloody marvellous, why don't you go out with him!
Maisy	Keep your voice down. Riverdale could be anywhere.
Tamsen	If they come near me, I'll give them a fight. More than that hopeless bunch would ever do.
Maisy	Riverdale could have knives Tam. Remember – they're the desperate underclass expressing themselves in the only way they know how.
Tamsen	I don't care. Bring them on. I'll tear their eyes out.
Maisy	Hugh Phillips has got lovely eyes.
Tamsen	Maisy you are *this* close…

Enter **Stanley**. *They see him. He doesn't see them. Beat.*

Maisy	Oh my sainted aunt. A prime cut Riverdale specimen.
Tamsen	Don't move.
Maisy	He's terrifying.
Tamsen	He hasn't spotted us. Look at him. Typical Neanderthal.
Maisy	So primitive. It's almost thrilling.
Tamsen	He's coming our way.

MAISY I'll make the owl-call. Then we'll run.

TAMSEN Don't you dare. We're dealing with this ourselves. What do you want… Riverdale scum? You want some action? You've come to the right place.

STANLEY I come in peace.

TAMSEN Very likely. One more step and you're white trash mincemeat.

STANLEY Homesleigh was built to celebrate the harmony of the spheres and the love of man and woman. I come to you in that spirit. I seek a member of St Nectan's who will walk with me through the garden. To defy the warring between Riverdale and St Nectan's that blights both our houses.

MAISY Tamsen I smell a weirdo.

TAMSEN Don't be so naive Maisy. It's a trap. He's trying to lower our guard. Look in the bushes for other eyes.

MAISY *(looking dramatically)* I can't see any.

STANLEY That's because there aren't any.

He approaches her and holds out his hand.

TAMSEN What do you think you are doing?

STANLEY I'm offering the olive branch.

TAMSEN The what?

STANLEY With this kiss I pledge peace to St Nectan's.

He kisses her on the cheek. **Tamsen** *immediately launches a martial arts attack on* **Stanley** *who is hurled to the ground.*

TAMSEN	What the hell do you think you're playing at? We're at war!
STANLEY	I don't believe in war.
TAMSEN	Shut up and get up and fight!
STANLEY	No.
TAMSEN	Get up!
STANLEY	I refuse!
TAMSEN	If you don't get up I'll kick you til you do.
STANLEY	Then kick me. I'm a pacifist. I'll do nothing.

She kicks him. He groans.

STANLEY	Told you.
TAMSEN	Get up will you! Be a man!
STANLEY	I don't want to.
TAMSEN	Christ are there no real men left in this world! Come on Mais… Let's get out of here…. Loser!

They leave. **Stanley** *is left on the ground.*

STANLEY	I won't be put off the path of peace! You won't put me off the path!

Enter **Cath** *and* **Billie**.

CATH	Haven't we done enough?
BILLIE	We've got to mark every cupid we find on the map with a red heart.
CATH	This is beyond moronic.

*They see **Stanley** on the ground*

CATH Stanley?

STANLEY Oh hi.

CATH Stanley are you all right?

She runs to him but he gets up and walks right past her.

STANLEY Billie did you see anybody from St Nectan's?

BILLIE No. Why?

STANLEY I have to find one of them. I have to keep going.

BILLIE Are you going to the ruckus?

STANLEY What do you think?

CATH Stanley's a pacifist Bill, I told you.

BILLIE Then why…

STANLEY Doesn't matter.

CATH Where you going?

STANLEY I said it doesn't matter!

And he runs off.

CATH He did it again. I am invisible.

BILLIE Forget him, he's a messed up saddo loser.

CATH I am one hundred per cent see-through.

BILLIE Come on. We've found twenty three cupids. Just seven to go and then we can have a fag. Now where could they be…?

*But as she speaks **Tamsen** and **Maisy** return.*

Cath	What do you want?
Tamsen	What do you think? The battle has begun.
Cath	Better get out your pompoms then hadn't ya?
Tamsen	What are you implying?
Cath/Billie	*(mock cheerleaders)* Go St Nectan's! Go St Nectan's!
Cath	I heard St Nectan's girls were made of fine China porcelain. Drop them and they smash.
Tamsen	Think again bitch.
Cath	What d'you call me?
Maisy	Tam, I'm not sure this is a good idea… These people are born into physical violence… It's in their blood…
Billie	Go on Cath. I'll take out the dwarf.
Maisy	I think she means me.
Tamsen	Go near her I kill you.
Cath	What you gonna do? Beat me to death with a violin bow?

***Cath** and **Tamsen** prepare to engage in battle. **Billie** approaches **Maisy**.*

Maisy	Tam. She's getting closer. I can smell her rage.
Tamsen	I'll keep them here. Sound the alarm.

***Maisy** tries to owl-call but can't.*

TAMSEN	Oh Christ's sake Maisy!
MAISY	My lips are shaking. I can't.
TAMSEN	Try again!
MAISY	I can't. I'm all moist!
TAMSEN	Run!
CATH	After her!

***Billie** chases **Maisy** out.*

TAMSEN	So it's just you and me. Let battle commence.
CATH	When I got here I wasn't much up for a ruckus. You girl have put me right in the mood.

***Tamsen** and **Cath** launch at each other but are suddenly stopped dead as **Cupid** comes alive.*

CUPID	Everywhere division
	Misunderstanding and misprision.
	Folks a fighting and a spitting
	And a hating and a hitting
	And no love they is a getting
	And the garden is a crying
	At this pain it is a spying
	It is so f...ing* mystifying
	How their lives they are wasting
	With this punching and a pasting
	How their hearts they are so sore
	For there ain't no love no more.

* To be pronounced 'effing', or as you wish.

>Now Cupid cast the spell
>
>To make the sick in love be well.
>
>And may this garden here present
>
>The shifting of the element
>
>Until all hate and anger gone
>
>Love rise in glory like the sun.

Cupid casts the spell.

>Now be changed in your look
>
>Swap the cover, keep the book

He casts his spell. **Tamsen** *and* **Cath** *have magically transformed clothes. They stare at each other.* **Cupid** *has returned to being a statue.*

CATH	What the…?
TAMSEN	What have you done? Give me back my uniform!
CATH	I didn't do anything! You took my clothes and somehow…
TAMSEN	Somehow what!
CATH	Somehow put yours on me…
TAMSEN	Oh yeah right that's really believable! Did you drug me? You did didn't you? With chloroform or one of those glues you lot are always sniffing… and then you tied me up and stripped me…
CATH	I did no such thing!
TAMSEN	Give them back chavess!
CATH	No way. Not until you give me mine!
TAMSEN	You think I want to wear this tat!

23

CATH	Take them off.
TAMSEN	I'm not taking my clothes off here. You take them off.
CATH	You first.
TAMSEN	No you. You!

*Enter **Hugh**, a boy from St Nectan's. Handsome.*

TAMSEN	Oh my God, it's Hugh Phillips. He mustn't see me. Hide me. Please.
CATH	In your dreams lady.
TAMSEN	I'll find you and I'll get you for this.

*Exit. **Hugh** sees **Cath**.*

HUGH	Hi Tamsen. Aren't you watching the barney?

Pause.

CATH	Sorry?
HUGH	It's starting any minute. Are you OK Tamsen?

Cath looks behind her. No one is there.

CATH	Uh... yeah...
HUGH	I asked if you were going to the barney.
CATH	Uh, I'm not sure I'm gonna bother.
HUGH	Nor me. I've nothing against Riverdale. *(embarrassed pause)* Look. About Saturday night. I wanted to say I'm sorry. I feel like such an idiot. *(**Cath** is silent)* Can we... I mean can we forget it ever happened?

Beat.

CATH	Sure.

HUGH	Maybe – give it another go…

Beat.

CATH	Sure.

HUGH	Thanks. I think the guys have got you all wrong. That's why I made such a fool of myself. I became convinced you were about to chuck me so I chucked you and it was stupid and… You were so upset… You were upset weren't you?

CATH	Yeah. *(she fakes a little 'upsetedness')* I mean it was hard…

HUGH	I know. I know. You tried to hide it, to act the hard nut. But I could tell… I'm sorry OK? *(he moves to hold her)* They all want me to take part in this stupid fight. I hate it, just because I'm a big guy and I work out and play football for the county, everyone expects me to be some kind of monster...

CATH	Yeah.

HUGH	So we'll give it another go?

CATH	If you like.

HUGH	Really?

They approach to kiss. Enter **Clive**.

CLIVE	Hugh. You're needed. The scabby bastards have filled their rucksacks with stones. Hi Tamsen.

Cath   Hi.

Clive   I thought you two had split…

Hugh   Who told you that?

Clive   You did. You said she was a seething pit of neuroses…

Hugh   Shut up Clive. Where are they?

Clive   Behind the grotto. It's getting out of control. I reckon we'll be chucked out if it goes on much longer. Come on daddio!

Hugh   *(to **Cath**)* I'd better show my face. See you later… Stay out of trouble… Sorry I didn't mean to tell you what to do.

Cath   No it's OK. (**Hugh** *kisses her and leaves with* **Clive**) OK this is weird.

My clothes are different.

But he thought I was… He thought I was…

She… She's tall and…

She's a stunner.

I'm a dog.

But even the other boy blushed when he looked at me.

No one has ever looked at me like that.

No one has ever touched me liked that.

Kissed me like that.

Who am I?

The lake!

*She looks in the mirror of the water. She sees **Tamsen**'s face mirroring hers.*

I'm her.

I'm so beautiful.

My legs go on forever.

My breasts defy all natural laws

My eyes are clear pools

My skin is polished marble

This is no ordinary garden.

*Enter **Stanley**, bloodied.*

Cath	Stanley? Are you OK?
Stanley	Keep away from me! I've already been kicked by you once!
Cath	What are you…?
Stanley	And now one of your school friends has beaten me up by the gothic waterfall. I went to shake his hand! He twisted my arm and smashed it against the rockery. Then like a coward he took some stones and invited his mates to take pop-shots! So forget it OK! My peace mission is over! Gandhi never had to suffer this!
Cath	Where are you going?
Stanley	I'm leaving the garden! I'm walking home. Where no one will meet me. Or talk to me. Or kick me. Or chop me. *(beat)* How did you know my name?
Cath	Um… I overheard it. Listen I'll come with you.
Stanley	No way. I don't want no St Nectan's anywhere near me. I just wanted to shake your hand! To make peace!

Cath	I'll shake your hand.
Stanley	No you won't!
Cath	I will.
Stanley	You won't. You know I'm a pacifist so you'll use that as a way to crap on me.
Cath	I won't. I promise.
Stanley	What about before?
Cath	What did I do?
Stanley	Don't pretend you don't know! Kicking a man when he's down!
Cath	That was me being a stupid dumb-arse posh cow. I've changed.
Stanley	That's a pretty sudden turnaround.
Cath	Yeah it is.

She holds out her hand.

Stanley	You serious?
Cath	Try me.
Stanley	You'll walk with me through the garden?
Cath	Yeah.
Stanley	And perform the peace, love and harmony action? You really want to?
Cath	More than anything in the whole world.
Stanley	You better not be having me on…
Cath	I'm not!

Stanley *tentatively takes her hand.*

STANLEY	This could be a major moment in our lives.
CATH	*(in heaven)* I do hope so.
STANLEY	The beginning of peace between Riverdale and St Nectan's.
CATH	Yes, of course.
STANLEY	What's your name?
CATH	Um… It's… It's Tam. Tamsen.
STANLEY	Walk with me Tamsen. Will you?
CATH	OK.
STANLEY	You know we're gonna get things thrown at us don't you?
CATH	I'd walk through arrows of fire for you.
STANLEY	You really have changed. Shall we…?
CATH	Yes. Let's walk in the garden.

Scene 4

Tamsen alone, hiding.

TAMSEN   What am I going to do?

I look like a member of the underclass.

Everyone is going to laugh at me.

Jocasta Mars Jones will piss herself.

Now she'll be the best looking girl in year ten.

I can't bear it!

I've got to take this off.

But then what – run through the garden in my underwear?

A horrible thought. She checks under her top.

Aaggh! What has she done to me?

The most awful cheap bra the world has ever known.

Oh some tropical bush come and swallow me up!

I just need to get out of here. Get home and change.

She feels her clothes.

My purse. She's got my purse!

How can I get back with no money?

I'll kill her! I'll tear her limb from limb!

I have to find her.

*Enter **Billie** running.*

BILLIE I lost her.

Pause.

    The dwarf. She ran into some azaleas. Did you do her?

TAMSEN Me?

BILLIE Yeah you, Cath – did you do the posh bitch? *(pause)* Hello, is there something wrong?

TAMSEN You're talking to me?

BILLIE No I'm talking to a tree, I'm just looking at you to confuse it. Of course I'm talking to you!

TAMSEN Who am I?

BILLIE Cath I know you're really down about Strange Stanley but I need you to pull through for me now OK? Did you give the St Nectan's bitch a beating?

Pause.

BILLIE I need to know! There are little beefs happening all over the place! HQ needs to know what's going on!

TAMSEN Yes. I mean yeah. Yeaaahhh.

BILLIE You are beautiful! I mean I know you're not actually beautiful. But you are beautiful!

TAMSEN What did you say?

BILLIE Nothing… I just…

TAMSEN I'm not beautiful?

BILLIE I didn't mean you're not... I meant that to me right now you are the most goddamned beautiful girl on the planet!

TAMSEN	Have you got a mirror?
BILLIE	Got a compact.
TAMSEN	That will do.

*She looks at herself in the compact. Sees **Cath**. Retches slightly.*

	Oh my God… Oh no. Oh no…
BILLIE	Oh Cath – I didn't mean it like that. Get a grip girl.
TAMSEN	Oh Jesus!
BILLIE	Cath – looks are paper thin.
TAMSEN	I'm hideous!
BILLIE	You're not man. You're sweet looking and you're kind.
TAMSEN	But my skin…
BILLIE	So you don't have skin like Scarlett Johanssen. Your mum lives next to a bypass and smokes four hundred cigarettes a day. It's not very Clarins is it? Cath – look at me. It's Billie. I'm your friend.
TAMSEN	Billie…
BILLIE	That's it babe. Look I know what you're going through. Your brother's all screwed up, your mum's depressed. The guy you like ain't exactly responsive. But you got mates. I'm your mate.
TAMSEN	Are you?
BILLIE	Course I am!
TAMSEN	Thanks Billie.
BILLIE	That's my girl. Now what we need to focus on is giving out some beef to those St Nectan's tossers. Am I right?

TAMSEN	You're right.
BILLIE	Hey! Welcome back to the party Catherine. We missed you while you were away.
TAMSEN	Billie? The guy I like…
BILLIE	Stanley…
TAMSEN	Stanley. He doesn't like me?
BILLIE	Well I think you know that babe. You have been in the same class for four years and he is yet to officially acknowledge your existence.
TAMSEN	He doesn't notice me.
BILLIE	You could dance naked in front of him with a feather sticking out your arse. I don't think he'd see it.

*Enter **Hugh** and **Clive**.*

HUGH	Stop right there.
TAMSEN	Oh my God.
CLIVE	Don't move slag.
TAMSEN	How dare you –
BILLIE	Yeah you take that back!
HUGH	We're not going to hurt you.
CLIVE	Aren't we? Why not?
HUGH	Clive please try and grow up.
CLIVE	This barrow boy punched me. I want payback!
HUGH	The fight has gone out of control up there. Someone's brought knives.

BILLIE	That would be the ammo…
HUGH	I'm warning you – for your own safety – keep away from the grotto.
BILLIE	Why should we believe you?
TAMSEN	Um… Billie wait.
CLIVE	Let's beat them up Hugh. Girls want equality, right? So that means we can beat the crap out of them, just like we do with boys.
BILLIE	Just you try it!
CLIVE	You're really getting on my tits.
BILLIE	What you gonna do about it? *(aside to **Tamsen**)* Let's split. I'll meet you at the bridge of Sighs. *(to **Clive**)* Come on dopey. Catch me.

*She exits. **Clive** chases after. Noises of fighting.*

HUGH	I don't want to fight OK?
TAMSEN	OK.
HUGH	There are hundreds of St Nectan's round here. We need to get you somewhere safe.
TAMSEN	The temple of Aphrodite is just down the hill.
HUGH	Perfect. What's your name?
TAMSEN	My name is Cath.
HUGH	Hugh. Hi.
TAMSEN	Hi.
HUGH	Come with me Cath.

Exeunt.

Scene 5

Cath and Stanley are walking hand in hand.

STANLEY — This is the grove of Apollo. From here we head up to the grotto. That's when we will begin the peace, love and harmony improvised action.

CATH — Do we have to go straight away?

STANLEY — You're not getting cold feet?

CATH — No I just thought… If we're going to do this, we need to know more about each other. They may try to divide us.

STANLEY — No, you're right. There must be no secrets between us. All right, what do you want to know?

CATH — I don't know… Just a bit about you…

STANLEY — My name's Stanley. I'm in Year Ten in…

CATH — No I know all that. I mean really about you. Why are you doing this? I mean it's great. But why?

STANLEY — I dunno. I just want to change something you know? I don't know if you'll understand.

CATH — Try me.

STANLEY — Have you ever been to Riverdale?

Beat.

CATH — No, never.

STANLEY — Well it's a dump right. Any kid whose parents give a toss has got out to St Nectan's or Gordon High, OK? So it's just the rest of us left here to rot. And what do we do? Nothing – we just pick

	fights, take drugs and piss our lives away. So anyway, I formed a club – to get people to think about how to make Riverdale better! It was after school on Wednesdays. First meeting – no one came.
CATH	That's not true!
STANLEY	What?
CATH	Sorry – I mean you were there.
STANLEY	Well of course I was there!
CATH	And was there no one else?
STANLEY	Well yeah there was this girl called Cath. But that was it.
CATH	And wasn't she worth having the club for?
STANLEY	She's just some messed up girl. Just came because she wanted some friends I reckon. Her mum's this... what's the word for when she don't leave the house...
CATH	Agoraphobic...
STANLEY	And her brother's in some young offenders prison. She just needed the company. So anyway, I cancelled the club there and then. Decided I was better as a lone operator.
CATH	What did Cath do?
STANLEY	Dunno.
CATH	Don't you think you might have hurt her feelings?
STANLEY	Maybe. Why you so obsessed with her?
CATH	But was there something wrong with her? Was she a real minger?

STANLEY	No. She's quite pretty.

Beat.

CATH	Is she?
STANLEY	Yeah. But she didn't look after herself. No self-respect. I mean I look at you. You look after yourself. You project an image.
CATH	But I've got money.
STANLEY	But there are people without money who do that. I was with this girl OK for a while. She was called Kelly.
CATH	Fisher.
STANLEY	You know her?
CATH	Through a friend.
STANLEY	Well Kelly right, she looks after herself. She projects self-respect.
CATH	My friend says she's a vain airhead.

Beat.

STANLEY	Yeah she is. I hated her really. But she projected an image. But Cath, right – she might be a diamond, but it's all hidden. What can I do with that?
CATH	Maybe she just needed a bit of a push. Maybe she's just like staggeringly, unbelievably unhappy and needs someone to bring her out of herself! I mean maybe.
STANLEY	Yeah, maybe. But I've had enough trouble doing that to myself, I ain't got time to be nobody's counsellor.

CATH   Oh Stanley…

STANLEY No don't say you know how I feel. Cos you don't.

CATH   What do you mean?

STANLEY St Nectan's is selective. I mean they say it's not, right, but it is.

CATH   Yeah.

STANLEY So you're chosen, right? You were selected. And that made you feel good. No one ever chose me. D'ya get it? What it feels like never to be chosen?

CATH   Yeah. I mean no.

STANLEY Like what you up to at the moment? In school.

CATH   Oh, you know, I'm getting ready for exams.

STANLEY Get straight As won't ya I bet? Everyone at St Nectan's gets straight As.

CATH   Probably.

STANLEY How many you taking?

CATH   Oh, sixteen.

STANLEY Sixteen?

CATH   Yeah. And then I'll do five A levels. Maths, further maths, even further maths, drama and politics.

STANLEY You into politics?

CATH   Yeah. Massively.

STANLEY Wow! I want to take politics. Thing is I reckon I'm going to fail all my GCSEs, which is a drawback.

CATH   Why you gonna fail?

STANLEY	I don't find Riverdale a very conducive learning environment.
CATH	But you're clever Stan. You shouldn't be failing at anything!
STANLEY	And then you'll go to University I bet.
CATH	Uni we call it.
STANLEY	Which one?
CATH	Well I'm lined up for Cambridge Uni but I might choose London Uni because I like to mix my academic work with living in a thriving urban scene.
STANLEY	What will you study there?
CATH	Politics, yeah. Specialising in the history of peaceful political protest.
STANLEY	They do a course in that? That's my dream course.
CATH	Martin Luther King. Mahatma Gandhi. And naturally we get to meet Nelson Mandela.
STANLEY	He's my hero!
CATH	He's going to talk to us about the problems of post-apartheid South Africa. It's going to be fascinating. And then I'm going to go into politics. Labour party probably though I reckon we need to take a long hard look at the whole party-political system which is rapidly becoming a joke.
STANLEY	You're amazing. Everything you say… I believe the only way forward is through…
CATH	Individual and collective action. Citizens joining together…
STANLEY	Spontaneous collective action…

Cath   Through real and online dialogue…

Stanley   To create a better…

Cath   And more loving world.

Pause.

Stanley   You're very beautiful. Your skin. It's like…

Cath   Polished marble.

Stanley   Your eyes are like…

Cath   Clear pools.

Stanley   I've never met anyone like you.

Beat.

Cath   I encourage you to individually act now Stanley.

He kisses her.

Stanley   No one at Riverdale kisses like that. That was… That was…

Cath   Shut up and do it again.

They kiss again

Cath   Let's walk.

Stanley   OK.

They take hands

Cath   Whatever happens, I will never let you go.

Scene 6

Maisy is crawling through the undergrowth.

MAISY I got away. Dived through a camellia bed and crawled round the temple of Flora. Two Riverdale boys were pinning a St Nectan's ninth year up against a statue of Vulcan. It was horrible. I just want to find somewhere quiet to finish *Middlemarch.* (*she almost literally bumps into* **Rock** *who is crawling in terror in the other direction. Both scream and recoil*) Aaaah!

ROCK Don't kill me! Please don't kill me!

Beat. They look at each other.

MAISY Are you from Riverdale?

ROCK Are you from St Nectan's?

MAISY Are you alone?

Rock nods.

ROCK You?

MAISY *(nods)* Are you going to shout for help?

ROCK Are you?

Beat.

MAISY What's your name?

ROCK My name is Tim but everyone calls me Rock.

MAISY Why do they call you Rock?

ROCK Because I'm the puniest boy in Riverdale. It's kind of a joke.

MAISY You shouldn't have told me that. I'm going to beat you up now. *(Beat.* **Rock** *gets scared)* That was a joke too.

ROCK Oh right.

MAISY Nice to meet you Rock. I'm Maisy.

ROCK What are you doing in the camellias?

MAISY I was trying to find somewhere to read.

ROCK Read what?

MAISY *Middlemarch*. It's a novel by George Eliot.

ROCK Never heard of him.

MAISY It's a woman. She writes about a nineteenth century woman who is trapped by her society into marrying for respectability rather than for love. George Eliot is my second favourite author. *(beat)* Aren't you going to ask who my favourite author is?

ROCK Go on then.

MAISY It's Jane Austen. My favorite book is *Emma*. And my favorite character is Mr. Knightley.

ROCK What's he like then?

MAISY He's quiet, unassuming and in some ways shy, but with an inner moral integrity that Emma finally finds irresistible.

ROCK I don't read books much.

MAISY I blame the decline of the lending library.

ROCK Just never really got into it.

MAISY	I could read to you.
ROCK	What, now?
MAISY	Neither of us want to fight. We could just stay here until it's time to go back to the coaches and I could read to you from *Middlemarch*.
ROCK	Suppose.
MAISY	Well I won't bother if you're not interested. God, you try to bring a bit of literature into their lives…
ROCK	No. I want to. It's just… If they see us…
MAISY	I'll say you were holding me hostage. You caught me and dragged me in here and roughed me up something dreadful.
ROCK	Really?

Maisy deliberately roughs up her uniform so it looks like she's been pushed around. This is oddly somewhat sexy.

MAISY	How's that? Vulnerable enough?
ROCK	It's great.
MAISY	You did that. You heathen. *(suddenly prosaic)* Come over here then. I won't bite. *(he approaches her cautiously)* We're nearly the same height.
ROCK	I hate being little.
MAISY	It's good for hiding under camellias. Now I'm already on chapter twenty seven so I need to start by giving you a summary of the story so far… Dorothea, a passionate young woman in search of a belief system to match the agitation of her mind, marries the dark and skeletal figure of Mr. Casaubon…

Scene 8

The temple of Aphrodite. **Hugh** *and* **Tamsen**.

HUGH You should be safe in here. It's quite a way from the main action.

TAMSEN Don't go yet.

HUGH I don't think we should be seen together.

TAMSEN Five minutes.

HUGH What do you want?

TAMSEN I don't know, just to spend some time together here in the temple of Aphrodite…

HUGH No, I think I should go.

TAMSEN Are you with anyone?

Beat.

HUGH Sorry?

TAMSEN Are you with a girl?

HUGH Why is that of any interest to you?

TAMSEN Oh. Because I'm in love with this boy at Riverdale, I mean this guy, and, right, I think he's well in love with me, man, but we keep messing it up big-style. So I thought, if you were with someone, you could maybe, I mean it would be well phat if you would help me out – tell me what to do.

HUGH I'm sort of with someone yes.

TAMSEN And that's just been very straightforward has it?

Hugh   No, not at all.

Tamsen   Well could you, I mean it would be well wicked man if you could tell me how you've tried to make it work.

Hugh   It's complicated. Tamsen…

Tamsen   Is that the girl's name?

Hugh   Yeah. She's incredibly insecure.

Tamsen   Is she?

Hugh   Yeah and she has no reason to be. She's beautiful and clever. But she has no faith in herself. Anyway I asked her out and she started playing these ridiculous games. She's done it with all the boys. It was like she was testing me or something.

Tamsen   I suppose when you're pretty, you might think that everyone is only interested in you physically. Innit.

Hugh   Exactly! It's as if her own beauty is destroying her! And I hate that! If God or Darwin or whoever gives you something, you should celebrate that!

Tamsen   But she uses it as a weapon to beat you with.

Hugh   Exactly! God you really get it.

Tamsen   So what did you do?

Hugh   Well, we went out on these first dates and it was just awful. It was like war. She hated everything, she didn't want to do anything. She acted appallingly really. So I chucked her.

Tamsen   And how did she take it?

HUGH	She broke apart. I've never seen anyone cry like that. And it was then I knew that somewhere inside this impossible stuck-up princess there was someone I could love. Really love.
TAMSEN	And who could love you.
HUGH	Yes. In fact we've just got back together.

Beat.

TAMSEN	You what?
HUGH	Yes just now at the Porch of Venus. She was wonderful.
TAMSEN	What do you mean?
HUGH	Amazing! Quite unlike her normal abhorrent behaviour. She was clever and sweet…
TAMSEN	Did you kiss her?
HUGH	Oh yeah. That's why I don't want to fight anyone. It's crazy. We're in this garden, it's a gorgeous day, Tamsen and I could be walking down a lakeside pathway or sitting under a tree…
TAMSEN	Yeah or equally we could be sitting here, in the temple of Aphrodite…
HUGH	We could be spending real time with each other.
TAMSEN	Holding each other. Kissing each other.
HUGH	Well, yes.
TAMSEN	Here.
HUGH	Instead we're in a war zone.

TAMSEN	Tell me something. Does her beauty really matter to you?
HUGH	Well, I like the way she looks.
TAMSEN	But say for a minute, say she wasn't beautiful. Say she was in the world's worst car crash and she was horribly disfigured.
HUGH	I don't really want to think about that.
TAMSEN	But you have to. If you really love someone, you have to know whether you would love them if their legs were cut off or their…
HUGH	I don't find that funny Cath.

Pause.

TAMSEN	I don't find it funny either.

She starts to cry.

HUGH	What is it?
TAMSEN	Nothing.
HUGH	I'm really sorry. Were you talking about… About yourself?

Tamsen *nods.*

HUGH	But you're pretty.
TAMSEN	I'm not! I'm disgusting!
HUGH	You're not!
TAMSEN	I am! I've seen myself. An ogress!

Hugh	Listen. Think about that boy you love. Think about him now.
Tamsen	Why?
Hugh	Just do it. Imagine he's right here in front of you.
Tamsen	OK.
Hugh	Are you doing it?
Tamsen	I'm doing it.
Hugh	You see? When you think of someone you love, you're beautiful.
Tamsen	Am I?
Hugh	Very. You have a quality. Almost like Tamsen's.
Tamsen	Really?

*They are close now. A moment's confusion. Broken by **Clive** who enters at pace.*

Clive	What are you doing?
Hugh/Cath	Nothing.
Clive	I've been looking for you everywhere. I was chasing the little mouthy one along the lakeside walk. You'll never guess what I saw.
Hugh	What?
Clive	Tamsen Adamsdale. Walking with a Riverdale boy. Hand in hand.

Beat.

Hugh	You can't have.

CLIVE	I swear on my life! And not just hand in hand. They…
HUGH	What?
Clve	Well you know, they were…
HUGH	They were what? They were WHAT CLIVE?
CLIVE	They were…

He mimes necking.

HUGH	Say it!

***Clive** whispers it to **Hugh**.*

HUGH	Not possible. Not possible.
CLIVE	Less than five minutes after you'd… *(mimes necking)*
HUGH	Take me to her.
TAMSEN	Hugh wait.
HUGH	Please Cath, this has nothing to do with you.
TAMSEN	But it does!
HUGH	IT HAS NOTHING TO DO WITH YOU!

*Exit with **Clive**. **Tamsen** bursts into tears.*

Scene 10

Stanley and Cath are walking together, hand in hand.

STANLEY OK, I think we should perform the peace, love and harmony improvised action here.

CATH What do we have to do?

STANLEY There are a series of mini peace actions that make up the complete action. I'm going to say some words, we hold hands, and we hug and kiss.

CATH Oh good. I mean… I just think that words are all very well… But actions really get the message across. We should probably practise… The kissing bit…

STANLEY I've kissed you seven times on this walk already.

CATH Just to be sure.

They kiss. Interrupted by Fraser running fast and bleeding.

FRASER Aaaaaghhhh! What the hell man!

STANLEY Fraze…

FRASER Have you not heard? Casey Phillips has been taken hostage by the St Nectan's boys. They're holding him in the grotto. They're demanding three Nokia phones as ransom. *(pause)* You were kissing her.

STANLEY Yes.

FRASER Stan we are in a serious ruck with this lot. Whose side are you on?

STANLEY On the side of peace, Fraze. I thought I'd made

	that clear.
FRASER	You cannot be on that side any more! We are getting them bastards! *(to **Cath**)* Your mates have taken my mate hostage.
CATH	How d'you know they're my mates?
FRASER	They're probably torturing him as we speak. So I reckon we need a hostage too!
STANLEY	Leave her alone Fraze.
FRASER	We need a hostage Stan and I'm looking at one right now!
STANLEY	I'm not giving her to you.
FRASER	I'll give you one more chance.
STANLEY	You're not taking her man.
FRASER	You're a twat, Stan.

*Fraser punches **Stanley**. He tries to grab **Cath** who launches an all-out assault on **Fraser**.*

FRASER	Get off man! Ow! Ow, get off! *(he retreats)* Bloody hell man. I thought posh girls were civilised!
CATH	Get with the programme dickhead. This kitten's got claws.
FRASER	All right all right! I don't want you as a hostage anyway!

Exit.

CATH	You all right?
STANLEY	Yeah. It's what we expected.

CATH   Your ribs are bruised.

STANLEY   It's OK. *(she kisses his ribs)* What you doing?

CATH   I admire you Stanley Arthur Peterson.

STANLEY   How did you know my middle name?

CATH   The same reason I know that your dad's a nutter who you do everything to avoid and your brother Shaun died in a fight outside a nightclub three years ago, and that in Shaun's name all you want in life is to stop the ruckus.

STANLEY   How did you know that?

CATH   By magic.

*She kisses him. Enter **Hugh** and **Clive**.*

CLIVE   There's the hussy!

STANLEY   What d'you want?

HUGH   How dare you?

CATH   Oh crap.

HUGH   How long ago was it Tamsen? Five minutes? Ten? You're sick in the head!

CATH   Hugh listen…

HUGH   People always said you were a liability. I didn't listen. I put my faith in you! I loved you!

STANLEY   Who is he?

CATH   I don't really know.

HUGH   You don't know! YOU DON'T KNOW! I'm your boyfriend Tamsen!

Stanley   Is he?

Cath   No!

Hugh   How can you say that?

Clive   She's a viper, Hugh. A double crossing anaconda!

Stanley   She says she was never your girlfriend.

Hugh   Then she's more evil than I thought. *(to **Cath**)* We went to see *Pride and Prejudice*! We kissed at the same time that the guy from *Spooks* kissed Keira Knightley! I bought you popcorn!

Cath   I've never seen *Pride and* whatever …

Stanley   You've got the wrong girl my friend.

Hugh   Don't tell me what girl I've got.

Stanley   She says she's never seen it and I believe her.

Hugh   Do you? And who are you, pray?

Clive   Yeah who are you?

Stanley   I'm a pacifist.

Clive   He's a what?

Stanley   Tamsen and I are performing a peace, love and harmony action here on Apollo's mound. Hit me and I won't respond.

Clive   What did he say he was?

Hugh   You won't respond?

Stanley shakes his head.

Cath   No don't Stan, not again.

Hugh hits him.

STANLEY   *(in agony)* See?

Pause. ***Hugh*** *leaves.*

CATH   Stan!

CLIVE   *(to **Stan**)* That'll teach you to be a pessimist.

Clive *hits him, not very hard.*

CATH   Get off him! I said get off you little bully!

She forces him back. Violently.

CLIVE   All right! Get off! It wasn't just me you know!

CATH   Piss off you maggot! *(**Clive** leaves. **Cath** returns to **Stanley**)* Oh Stan.

STANLEY   Are you still with me Tamsen?

CATH   I'm still here.

STANLEY   Don't go Tam, please. I don't think I could bear it if you went now.

CATH   I'm not going. I'm not going.

She holds him.

Scene 11

Tamsen alone in the temple of Apollo. **Hugh** *enters, sits despondently apart.*

Tamsen   What is it?

Hugh   Nothing. Nothing.

He starts to fight back the tears.

Tamsen   Are you OK?

Hugh   Just leave me alone please.

Tamsen   What happened?

Beat.

Hugh   Do you ever think you're just not made out for having a successful relationship?

Tamsen   Yes quite often.

Hugh   There are lots of girls who want to go out with me.

Tamsen   I know there are.

Hugh   But I don't want them! I want the lunatic! The self-destructive, insane madwoman.

Tamsen   You mean Tamsen…?

Hugh   She was kissing him. In broad daylight!

Tamsen   Kissing who?

HUGH   This Kevin. Utterly shameless. There's no way she can really fancy him. She's just doing it to screw us up.

TAMSEN   I'm sure that's not true.

HUGH   You don't know her. She has a perverse evil streak. There's nothing she'd like more than to twist a dagger in my heart.

TAMSEN   Don't say that.

HUGH   You know my problem? My parents are too sorted. I have to find someone crazy and unreliable just so I'm not like them. I'm too reliable!

TAMSEN   I love that about you.

HUGH   You don't know me.

TAMSEN   No, of course. But in our time together. I think you're a wonderful person.

HUGH   Do you think so?

TAMSEN   I know so.

Beat.

HUGH   The boy you like. Is he reliable?

TAMSEN   Yes.

HUGH   Hold on to him. Marry him immediately

TAMSEN   I'm not sixteen yet.

HUGH   Book it for your sixteenth birthday. The world is full of insane maniacs. A decent human being is gold dust!

TAMSEN	The thing is… I can't… Marry him…
HUGH	Why not?
TAMSEN	Because… Because something happened. Here today. In the garden.
HUGH	What?
TAMSEN	You'll think I'm insane. You won't believe me.
HUGH	Of course I will.
TAMSEN	Well what happened was… *(beat)* I've found someone else… someone even better. Even more amazing.
HUGH	Who?
TAMSEN	Someone here in the garden.
HUGH	I don't know what you mean.
TAMSEN	Someone in this temple. Right here. Right now.

Pause.

HUGH	You mean… Me?
TAMSEN	Well it's either you or that statue of Hercules.
HUGH	But Cath. It's not possible.
TAMSEN	Why? Because we're from different schools?
HUGH	Well yes. I mean… No… I mean.
TAMSEN	You said I was pretty.
HUGH	And you are… But…
TAMSEN	It's a class thing.

Hugh	No, it's just…
Tamsen	You wouldn't know what to say to your parents.
Hugh	Cath, what are you talking about? We don't know each other!
Tamsen	But we do! *(she grabs him)* Look at this temple. Look at the carvings. They're all kissing, making love. They don't think about what their parents will think!
Hugh	But I don't love you! I love Tamsen!
Tamsen	I am Tamsen!

Beat.

Hugh	It's happening again. Another wacko.
Tamsen	Sorry I…
Hugh	Just get away from me please.
Tamsen	Don't go!
Hugh	Get off me! *(she tries told on to him! He throws her off)* Get lost!

*Exit. **Tamsen** gets up off the ground.*

Tamsen	I'm not losing you. I'm not losing you!

She follows him out. A siren sounds. A voice travels through the garden.

Voice	This is Garden Security. Will all Riverdale and St Nectan's pupils make their way immediately to the exit of the garden. Make your way to the exit of the garden.

Scene 12

Billie and *Fraser* meet at Cupid's Gate.

Fraser   What happened?

Billie   Garden Security found out about the ruckus. They're chucking us out.

Fraser   Ah man! We were only just kicking off!

Billie   I've been trying to find my way to the exit. It's a nightmare – there are cupids everywhere. It's like they're multiplying or something!

Fraser   Have you seen Stanley?

Billie   No why? He's not on one of his peace binges again is he?

Fraser   Big style. He was kissing this slag from St Nectan's on the mound of Apollo. Said it was an olive branch.

Billie   He's cracked that bloke.

Fraser   I hit him Billie. My own mate.

Billie   I haven't seen Cath for half an hour. We were cornered by these two guys. I don't know if she made it. She was having a real crisis.

Fraser   What about ?

Billie   You know what about? Your pacifist friend. She's head over heels.

Fraser   Beats me why.

Billie   I don't get boys.

Fraser   I don't get girls.

BILLIE	I get girls.
FRASER	You are a girl.
BILLIE	But I actually get girls. Doesn't matter.
FRASER	What do you mean? You mean… You don't mean…?
BILLIE	Give it up Fraze.
FRASER	I don't get boys.
BILLIE	It's all right Fraze I won't tell.
FRASER	I'm not gay!
BILLIE	Your secret's safe with me.
FRASER	I AM NOT GAY!

*Enter **Hugh** followed by **Tamsen**.*

HUGH	Will you please get your friend off my back.
TAMSEN	I am Tamsen! I'm not letting you go.
BILLIE	Cath?
TAMSEN	I'm not Cath!
BILLIE	Oh God she's really lost it.
TAMSEN	I love you Hugh. You can do what you want with me. Beat me, use me as your spaniel, I am not letting go!
HUGH	I just want to get out of here!
BILLIE	That's what we've been trying to do. We keep coming back to the same place.

Hugh	What nonsense! I've never heard such rubbish. *(he makes to leave.* **Tamsen** *grabs on)* Out of my way – you spotted toad!

Exit **Hugh**. **Tamsen** *starts to weep.*

Billie	Cath… Please calm down…
Fraser	She's a basket case.
Billie	Cath… It's just all the pressure you've been under. Your mum, your brother… You need to go and talk to someone.
Tamsen	I AM NOT CATH! My name is Tamsen Summers. I am in year ten at St Nectan's. I am beautiful and leggy and witty and wonderful and that prick is in love with me but he can't see it!

Pause.

Billie	Fraze I think we might need to get Mrs Gunnasekara.
Tamsen	I am not in your school! I am not in your class! I am not one of you!!

Enter **Clive**.

Clive	Oh no.
Tamsen	Clive, come here.
Clive	How do you know my name? You're freaking me out.
Tamsen	This is Clive Marshall. He's in year ten and he sits next to Hugh Phillips and behind Caroline Kendall because he fancies her but she thinks

he's a dork. He has a far more talented brother called Giles who is prefect at the school and who plays the oboe. Now can you see that I am not Cath. I am TAMSEN. I am ME!

CLIVE   Get away from me, you witch!

*Enter **Stanley**, bleeding, and **Cath**.*

FRASER   There he is! Stan.

STANLEY   Keep away from me.

BILLIE   What happened?

CATH   The siren came and the ruckus was over. The St Nectan's and Riverdale boys saw us – they thought it was us that had snitched on them. Both schools came together and turned on us. They threw Stanley in the lake. Then they dragged him out and punched him and kicked him. There were thirty of them. The cowards!

FRASER   Stan I'm sorry.

CATH   So you should be!

BILLIE   Shut it you rich bitch. Just because money comes out of your arse...

CATH   Money doesn't come out of anywhere!

STANLEY   None of you understand. She is the only one who tried to break the stranglehold of history. Together we stood up and defied the enmity and hatred between the schools. You despised us for that and you took us down. Ours is the victory. Ours is the... *(he calls out to the garden)* Gather around all you from St Nectan's and Riverdale. Come and join us here at Cupid's Gate. Put down your arms!

The schools gather.

>My name is Stanley Noble. This is Tamsen Summers of St Nectan's. Together we tried on the mount of Apollo to complete the peace, love and harmony action. You threw stones at us. You threw me into the lake of Hesperus. But we are still here. Now together we will perform the action and YOU WILL LISTEN! *(he turns to* **Cath***)* You ready?

Cath Yes.

Stanley/Cath We met today in the garden.

>We saw beneath the clothes
>
>We saw deeper than skin
>
>We are in love
>
>From differing houses
>
>We are in love
>
>From warring factions
>
>We are in love
>
>Though they hurl bricks at our heads
>
>We are in love
>
>Though they cast us into pits
>
>We are in love
>
>Though they kill our bodies
>
>Our souls are intertwined.

They kiss. Silence.

Stanley That's it. It's done.

Billie That was beautiful Stan.

CLIVE	Wow. That was actually kind of amazing.
STANLEY	Thanks.

Hugh enters.

HUGH	I hate this garden!
TAMSEN	Hugh!
HUGH	GET HER AWAY FROM ME! *(he turns and sees **Cath**)* Just tell me. Tell me truthfully. Who do you love?
CATH	I love him.
HUGH	But look at him.
CLIVE	Love knows no boundaries.
HUGH	What?
BILLIE	Their love has bridged the divide between our two schools.
FRASER	Yeah we don't want to fight no more.
HUGH	Have you all gone mad? That's my girlfriend!
TAMSEN	I'm your girlfriend! I'M YOUR GIRLFRIEND! I'M YOUR GIRLFRIEND! I'm Tamsen Summers! *(**Tamsen** turns to **Cath**)* Tell them.
CATH	Tell them what?
TAMSEN	Tell them what happened. At the Porch of Venus.
CATH	Nothing happened.
TAMSEN	You are not me! You are not from St Nectan's!
CATH	That's bollocks!

TAMSEN	All right. Who do you sit next to in geography?
CATH	I'm not answering your questions!
TAMSEN	Clare Wyatt and Tara Willoughby. What's the name of the physics teacher?
CATH	Get lost will ya?
TAMSEN	Mr. Hemment. Who won the victor ludorum for the long jump at the school sports day?
CATH	…
TAMSEN	He did! Hugh Phillips. And I'm his love! I'm Tamsen Summers.
BILLIE	Cath have you been spying on St Nectan's?
TAMSEN	I AM NOT CATH! SHE IS!

*Enter **Cupid** from the Gate.*

CUPID	Now maybe I should clear up the confusion.
FRASER	What the…
CUPID	You schools were brought here today for a reason.
	To sort your troubles and to cure your beefing.
	The police and the council were at a loss
	Pupil referral units couldn't give a toss.
	They asked the gods of love to intervene
	Venus gave me a call and here's the scene
	I took the soul of one and switched it round
	Gave Tam the form of Cath and Cath to Tam
	Now warring ceases and love rules the day
	And you have seen that you are not to blame

> That while St Nectan's overflows with dosh,
> And thus is like a magnet to the posh
> Riverdale declines and is forgot
> Like a poor cousin that you wished was not
> Now Cath be Cath and Tam be Tam again
> And everything will be as right as rain.

*Cupid switches them round. **Tamsen** is back in her ordinary clothes. **Cath** too. Immediately **Stanley** goes to **Tamsen**.*

BILLIE	Like what the hell happened there?
STANLEY	Tamsen?
TAMSEN	No. I mean I am Tamsen. But I'm not the girl you… She is.
STANLEY	What are you saying? I've been kissing you all afternoon.
TAMSEN	No you haven't.
STANLEY	I know who I kissed!
TAMSEN	You kissed my body, but her soul.
STANLEY	I don't believe you!
CUPID	Kiss both and then my friend you'll know. Who has the body and who the soul?
HUGH	Why should he kiss my…?
CUPID	Sssshhh. Stop fretting frat boy.

*Stanley kisses **Tam**. He goes over and kisses **Cath**. This kiss becomes longer. And longer. They stop.*

STANLEY	You. It was you all along.

CATH	I'm sorry Stan.
STANLEY	I did the peace, love and harmony action with a girl from my own class. We did not bridge no divide.
CATH	But it worked Stanley. Everyone stopped fighting. Look around you.
STANLEY	A hollow gesture! It will all start again!
BILLIE	No, it won't!
CLIVE	No way Jose. We're all pessimists now.
FRASER	They're right Stan. You did it. I'm through with the ruckus.
HUGH	Does that mean. Cath was…
TAMSEN	Cath was me.
HUGH	In the temple of Venus…
TAMSEN	Yes.
HUGH	The light in your eyes. When you thought of the boy you loved.
TAMSEN	It was you.

They hug.

STANLEY	But don't you see? We're just as we were! I'm with her and she's with you! Nothing has changed at all.
CUPID	Then now one final revelation
	Before I flee back to my station.

Cupid *reveals* **Maisy** *and* **Rock** *kissing in the camellias. They do not see us.*

MAISY   If we don't stop kissing I won't be able to get to the end of chapter sixty two. And it's a corker.

ROCK   Sorry. Go on.

MAISY   *(begins to read)* "She sank into the chair and for a few moments sat there like a statue, while images and emotions were hurrying upon her. Joy came first – joy in the impression that it was really herself whom Will loved…"

ROCK   Just one more.

MAISY   God, you working classes are insatiable…

They kiss. Everyone laughs. They turn to see the entire school.

MAISY/ROCK   Aaaah!

TAMSEN   What are you doing Maisy Haggard?

MAISY   Nothing. He's been holding me hostage. Honest he has. He's been brutal. Physically keeping me against my will.

FRASER   Yeah, looks like it.

MAISY   I know he looks weedy, but when he's angry – you don't want to know what he's capable of!

TAMSEN   It's OK Maisy. No one's going to beat either of you up.

ROCK   You're not going to whack me?

STANLEY   No Rock. You two are the legacy we need. You are the meeting of Riverdale and St Nectan's!

ROCK   Are we?

STANLEY   You have performed the peace, love and harmony action! Kiss her.

Cath	Kiss her!
All	Kiss her!
Rock	Really? OK.
Maisy	Oh shucks.

They kiss. Everyone claps.

Tamsen	Lead us back to the coaches Maisy.
Stanley	And anyone can go on any coach they like!
Fraser	I bet theirs has got telly.
Clive	It has actually. And DVD.
Fraser	I'm going in theirs.
Clive	But they only play wildlife videos.
Fraser	Ah man, that is so unfair.
Maisy	It's the down-side of privilege.
Stanley	Let's go!
Cupid	Lovers join hands.
	Time to exit the gate
	And head for the carriages
	That solemnly wait.
	The journey is long
	There is much to discuss
	So get out of the garden
	And head for the bus!

The two schools parade out, hand in hand.

End

Staging the play

THE SETTING

Think about the opening of the play. We find ourselves, as Stanley tells us, 'at the entrance to Homesleigh – one of the great 18th century English landscape gardens'. Clues about the style of this garden are supplied by Stanley, who reads from his activity pack:

> **Stanley** Stand at the entrance to the garden and look before you at the artificial lakes carved out of the landscape, Romanesque temples and statues dotted amidst abundant flora and shrubbery and the statues of Aphrodite, goddess of desire, and Apollo, god of unity and harmony.

The temples and statues suggest that this is a neoclassical garden. Neoclassicism was a revival style, inspired by the art and architecture of Ancient Greece and Rome, which became fashionable in the gardens of large stately homes in 18th century England.

This style contrasted sharply with the typically formal 17th century gardens that preceded it. The two pictures below illustrate the difference:

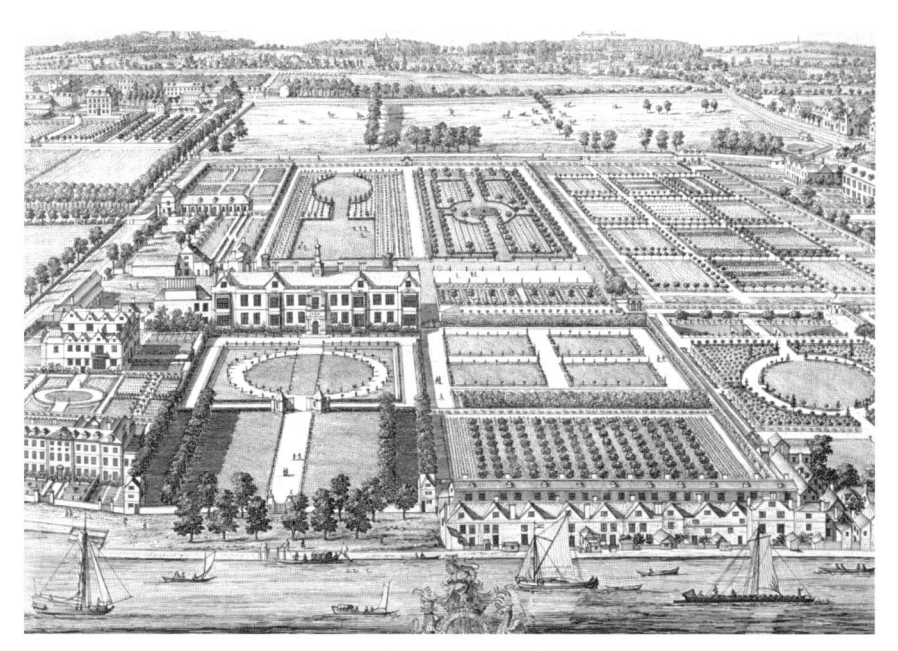

Aerial view of the Duke of Beaufort's seat in Chelsea, 1720.

View of the Lake at Stourhead, Wiltshire, 1790.

The great gardens of the 17th century were – as the first image shows – ornate, extravagant and laid out in precise mathematical patterns. The foremost exponents of this 'ultra-civilised' style were the Italians and the French. The most famous gardener was Andre Le Note, who designed the gardens at Versailles for Louis XIV.

In contrast, the English landscape movement aspired to a more 'natural' look. In these gardens:

- Lines are curved and meandering.
- There are a series of 'informal' vistas or views punctuated by focal points in the form of classical temples, ruins, and benches.
- Lawns come right up to the house, often at the expense of any regular flower garden.
- Plantings were of different height, shape, and colour: trees and shrubs were used to construct a balanced view and lines of sight.
- The garden is opened up to the surrounding parkland, and the parkland becomes a part of the garden scheme. This is often achieved by using a 'ha-ha', or hidden ditch.

Ha-has are still found in the grounds of grand country houses and estates and act as a means of keeping the cattle and sheep in the pastures and out of the formal gardens, without the need for obtrusive fencing. The word ha-ha came about because people came across the ditch unexpectedly and the surprise caused them to exclaim 'Ah! Ah!'.

Gardening in the 18th century was not just a private activity or hobby. It was the ground on which philosophical, aesthetic and scientific debates were waged. The writers Richard Addison and Alexander Pope were amongst those agitating for a change from the stifling formality of the 17th century garden. At the same time, Sir Joseph Banks, director of the

Royal Botanic Gardens at Kew, was building up a collection of exotic plant specimens shipped from as far a-field as South America, New Zealand and Australia for scientific research.

Stourhead Garden, pictured above, is very similar to the imaginary garden of Cecil Fortescue described in the play. When Henry Hoare II inherited the Stourhead estate in 1725 he began a wildly ambitious project to transform its grounds. Inspired by his visits to Italy, he hired an architect to build temples and features that reminded him of the classical and Renaissance remains he had seen in Rome. These included a grotto, a temple to Apollo and a temple to Flora, a Palladian Bridge, and, most extravagantly, a model of the Pantheon. Statues of the classical gods were scattered throughout. In his quest for authenticity, Hoare went so far as to import volcanic lava, limestone and tufa from Italy!

Hoare had a line from Virgil's epic poem, *The Aeniad*, inscribed in one of his temples. It read: 'Begone, you who are uninitiated! Begone'. There is a funny contrast between this line and the opening of *Ruckus in the Garden*. Apart from Stanley, the pupils of Riverdale Comprehensive show very little interest in the classical features of Homesleigh Garden. Nor are they the type of person, perhaps, that Henry Hoare would have imagined roaming his land. Much of the play's humour derives from this contrast between the classical, harmonious setting and the teenage characters who temporarily inhabit it, intent on their planned ruckus, 'Three pm in the temple of Apollo' (p.8). Despite this, the garden and the mythical figures it contains gradually exert their effect over the teenagers as the drama is played out.

You can research Stourhead Garden further using the website listed at the end of this book.

SET DESIGN

Once you are familiar with the style of 18th century gardens you will be able to use elements of your research to design the set for your play. You will have several choices available. You could decide to use real plants and shrubs in pots to suggest a realistic garden. You may find that you could borrow these from your local garden centre for your production in return for a programme credit. If you do this, don't forget to water them and ensure they get enough light. You should arrange them onstage so that they best facilitate the staging: for example, choose a suitable plant or row of plants that represent the camellias behind which Maisy and Rock become intimate towards the end of the play.

You may however decide to go for a non-realistic representational look. You could peruse the paintings of Henri Rousseau who had a particular way of painting foliage. Notice how his flat use of colour with little attempt to create perspective results in a depiction of landscape, which is dense with mystery. The set design for *Ruckus* could comprise two-dimensional cut-outs around the stage of painted representations of topiary.

You could opt for a monochrome version of the last suggestion. Look at eighteenth century pen and ink drawings of houses and gardens. They are almost diagrammatic. In black and white your set would prove a good background for the comic antics of the actors if they wore colourful costumes.

The most important thing to remember about the garden when doing your research is that it was once a place which only a privileged few could enjoy, whereas it can now be experienced by anyone who can afford the admission price.

Making a Ground Plan

When you have decided on your set design, you should draw a scale ground plan for it with every item marked clearly on it.

This should then be taped out on the rehearsal room floor before each rehearsal so the actors become familiar with the dimensions of the acting space and the whereabouts of all the elements of the set.

Consider this example of a ground plan for Mike Leigh's play, *Two Thousand Years*, staged in the Cottesloe theatre at the National.

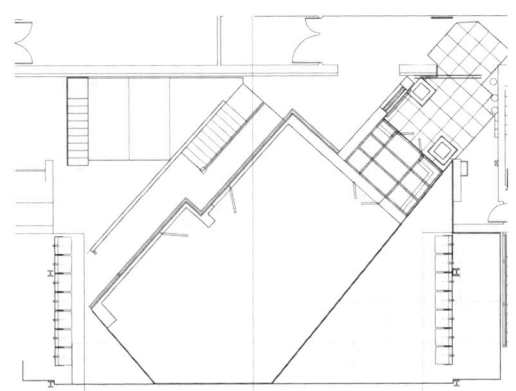

Imagine what this set design must look like from the auditorium. It is a realistic representation of an English living room in North London. See if you can work out the walls, staircases, where the actors can entrance and exit and where they can move about in the action.

COSTUME

It is important that you don't use your own school uniform as when watching the play the audience must be transported into another world that has its own truth and logic. Once you have decided upon the school uniforms for the two schools, each actor should be encouraged to adapt, adorn and wear their uniform as they think the character would: for example, how would they wear their tie? Stanley may wear peace movement badges. Would the girls wear excessive make-up? Would they wear outdoor coats? Hoodies? Scarves of their favourite football team?

Cupid

Roman god of love, counterpart to the Greek god of love Eros, Cupid is the son of Venus. The most popular representation of Cupid is as a cherubic boy usually having wings and holding a bow and arrow, symbolizing the love he bestows upon couples who deserve it.

See how many images of Cupid you can find. Print them off and hang them up on your ideas wall.

You should then go about designing a costume for the actor who is going to play Cupid. You could paint the actor a certain colour so that he looks like a stone statue. Or you could use a body stocking which has been dyed the desired colour. Remember that the actor has to be able to stand completely still for a significant amount of time, and then be able to move easily. How will they get onto the stage for the scenes that they are in? Perhaps they are wheeled on standing on a small plinth which has wheels underneath so that the illusion that they are a statue is sustained from the moment they are first seen until the first moment that they 'come to life'.

THE PHYSICAL CHALLENGES OF STAGING

Transformations and Reveals

You need to find practical ways of solving the moments of magic in this play.

There are moments of visual revelation which are magical: these are known in theatre as **reveals**. Then there are times when characters or circumstances are transformed: these are called **transformations**. Cupid is transformed from a stone statue into a living creature who is able to speak to the other characters and the audience. He will probably be played by an actor, or perhaps many actors. You may decide to interpret the character of Cupid as some sort of puppet. Then there is the crucial scene in which Tam and Cath swap their identities. They need to exchange costumes, and perhaps also hairstyles and any jewelry, spectacles etc. David Farr has written Cupid's speech into this sequence to help cover this change. It would be best if this were to take place in full view of the audience.

Staging experiment: using doubles

One way you could achieve the transformation is to use doubles of these two characters. This means two other actors are used to play Tam and Cath while they change their costume. In suitable lighting, the girls could walk around passing behind bushes, perhaps whilst some music is playing. As soon as possible switch the real actors for the doubles who continue to walk amongst the shrubs and then switch back to the real actors once they have completed their quick change. This requires detailed staging and rehearsal. If the actors are backlit and rarely show their faces to the audience it is possible to pull this trick off in a way which will convince the audience that Cupid has worked his magic.

Unarmed Combat and Slapstick

There are some sequences of physical action in this play, which although straightforward require careful rehearsal so that no one is injured. Take for example the stage direction on page 18:

> He kisses her on the cheek. **Tamsen** immediately launches a martial arts attack on **Stanley** who is hurled to the ground.

It is important that the actor playing Tamsen is positioned downstage of Stanley at this moment so that she can present the action to the actor playing Stanley and not actually touch him, though it will look from the audience's perspective as though she has done as his reaction will be timed precisely in order to indicate this. For safety it is worth the actor who is delivering the martial arts action firstly stretching her hand, and perhaps leg, in slow motion, as if sizing Stanley up. What the actor is actually doing is physically measuring the space between her and her victim in order to ensure that when she lashes out in real time, she is able to throw the movement within millimetres of his body, without actually touching him.

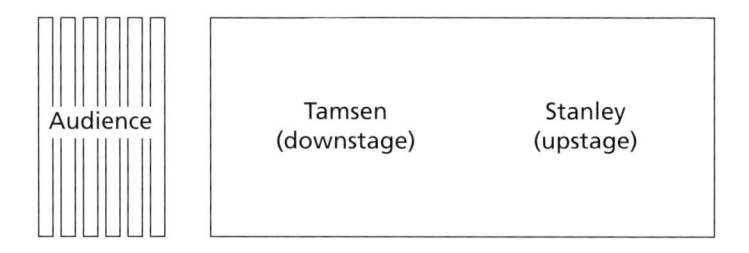

```
┌─────────────────────────────────────────┐
│                                         │
│                                         │
│         Tamsen            Stanley       │
│       (downstage)        (upstage)      │
│                                         │
│                                         │
└─────────────────────────────────────────┘
  Audience
```

The appropriate reactions of the other characters are also important in convincing the audience that an act of violence has taken place. What would Maisy's reaction be to this? Timing of course is crucial. All movement and reactions should be carefully rehearsed so that the actors have them in their 'muscle memory' and are able to deliver them with confidence.

A similar trick can be employed for the kicking of Stanley whilst he is on the ground. If the actor lies with his face and belly facing upstage out of sight of the audience, offering an empty palm to the top of Tamsen's foot, she will be able to feign kicking with force, whereas actually what she does is to clap the soft top of her foot into Stanley's hand. Again Stanley should react with his whole body to complete the effect as he groans.

🎵 MUSIC

Although there is no specific music mentioned in the script, you may want to occasionally use music in your production of the play. George Frederic Handel and Thomas Arne were prominent composers at the time when the garden of Cecil Fortescue was built. You may find it effective to use a combination of eighteenth century music and contemporary music that the characters in the play listen to, like rock or indie.

Recorded music could be used to accompany transitions of scenes, to help change the mood appropriately, or to show that certain amount of time has passed. You may also want to use music during sequences of transformation and magic. Or you may decide to use music underneath some spoken dialogue in order to heighten it and mark special moments. For example, an eighteenth century piece of music could be played quietly under Stanley's first speeches to help create a picture of the garden in the audience's imaginations.

You may want to align certain tracks of music, period or contemporary, to certain characters, for their entrances and exits. This will enhance their identities by giving the audience an idea of the sort of music they may listen to.

When you come to bring to life the character of Cupid, you may want to accompany his first speech with some magical chords, or invent a rhythm to accompany his speech in the style of rap or hip-hop.

Rhythm

Look at the rhythm of the beginning of his first speech and experiment with different ways of reciting each line. Which words would you stress? Underline or highlight those words. Where would you put pauses? How would you make the most of the rhyme scheme in this speech?

cont'd

> **Cupid** Everywhere division
> Misunderstanding and misprision.
> Folks a fighting and a spitting
> And a hating and a hitting
> And no love they is a getting
> And the garden is a crying
> At this pain it is a spying
> It is so f…ing mystifying
> How their lives they are wasting
> With this punching and a pasting
> How their hearts they are so sore
> For there ain't no love no more.
>
> (page 22)

SOUND

Think about the use of the security voice towards the end of the play. Might this sound like Big Brother or a similar sinister character who would be familiar to the audience. Perhaps the voice could be provided by a known adult with a role of seniority.

LIGHTING

The crucial thing to remember when designing lighting for comedy is that it needs to be bright. Actors' faces must be well lit at all times. It is possible to create shady parts of the garden by using leaf gobos in lanterns which can project them (see examples below), but you should always have a good general wash on the areas where essential stage dialogue and business is taking place.

Gobos always look better when they are projected onto the floor and light actors as they walk through them. This simulates what happens when the sun shines through foliage. Don't worry about 'showing' the effect of the gobo projected, the effect is at its best when it hits people because they are three dimensional and moving. Gobos tend not to look so good when projected onto flats, walls, curtains or scenery.

CHARACTERS

David Farr has chosen the names for his characters with affection and acuteness. There are names which may typically be associated with privileged classes, for example, Hugh and Clive. Then there are names which are ironic as they don't typify the personality of the character, like Rock, who is not hard, solid or secure as his name would suggest…

>   **ROCK**   I don't like fights Stan.
>
>   **STANLEY**   Nor do I Rock.
>
>   **ROCK**   Yeah but you disapprove for moral and political reasons. I just get really scared.

Rock's journey through the play reaches completion when he gets to know St Nectan's pupil, Maisy, whose ideal man is Mr. Knightley from Jane Austen's novel *Emma*. It becomes apparent when she describes her hero in the novel that she is also describing Rock:

> He's quiet, unassuming and in some ways shy, but with an inner moral integrity.

How might this relate to his name?

It is no accident that names are ascribed to certain personalities in drama. Writers often spend a lot of time thinking carefully about the names they give their characters.

Discussion

Discuss in class what might have inspired David Farr's choice of names. Might he have been influenced by the names of famous people who have similar personas to the ones he was creating? For example, actors like Hugh Grant and Billie Piper pictured here.

Writing

It would be interesting for you to find out from your family where the idea for your name came from. Write a paragraph on the story of your name. Were you named after a grandparent or other relative? You should also draw your family tree indicating the names of all the other members of your family.

Themes within and around the play

LANGUAGE IN THE PLAY

Contemporary Language

Ruckus

The 'South Sea Bubble' of 1720 (the year the garden was built) was one of the worst great stock market crashes. Alexander Pope details these events in his poem 'The South Sea Ballad', which he wrote to his friend Fortescue. In it he refers to that particular ruckus as a squabble and a rabble.

The word RUCKUS itself seems to date from 1890, and is possibly a blend of ruction and rumpus. It is sometimes shortened to RUCK. The *Oxford English Dictionary* defines it as:

> An uproar, a disturbance; a row, a quarrel; fuss, commotion.
>
> *Oxford English Dictionary Online*

Have a look at the full O.E.D. definition yourself. In what contexts has the word been used?

> **Discussion**
>
> How many other words can you think of that have the same meaning as RUCKUS?

83

Language

Make a list of other words in the play which you would describe as contemporary teenage-speak. Try and find out the history of these words and how they came into spoken language.

You should make a list of words by going through the script page by page. Include all words you think may be considered slang or informal. Begin by looking them up in a dictionary or thesaurus. Talk about what sort of people are likely to use them and which speakers will not use them. You should also discuss where they are likely to be heard and where they are not.

Draw a table to record your findings which could look like this:

Ruckus in the garden glossary				
Word	Other words with same meaning	History	People likely to use it	Places likely to hear it spoken
Toff				
Puking				
Lick	Beat, win over			
Ammo		Short for ammunition		
Chav				
Scum				
Minger	Unattractive			
Loose canon				
				Boys
				Playground

Gang Warfare

What other plays, stories or films can you think of which are about rival gangs? What similarities can you identify between those and *Ruckus in the Garden*? How do these gangs behave?

84

How did the boys' attempts at social organisation descend into tribal warfare in William Golding's novel, Lord of the Flies?

Why do you think Baz Luhrmann decided to set his version of Romeo and Juliet *in the feuding gang life of contemporary Los Angeles?*

Gangs often have elaborate systems of dress, belief and behaviour. The famous LA gangs, the Bloods and the Crips, marked themselves out by what they wore. The Crips were known in the 1970s by their black leather jackets (in homage to the Black Panthers), earrings worn in the left earlobe, and by the canes they carried.

85

Although they came to be known for their violent crimes, the original 'Crib' gang had a political dimension. Its founder member, 15 year-old Raymond Washington, hoped to continue the revolutionary momentum of the Black Panther movement, after the party had been suppressed by the US authorities for its subversive activities in the late 1960s.

Another US gang, the Kings, circulates its own manifesto, detailing the significance of its symbol, a three pointed crown, and its black and gold colours. It also provides a philosophy of social justice, named the Code of Kingism, as well as helpful advice for how to choose a lawyer or survive in prison should you end up on the wrong side of the law.

Thinking of your own examples from fiction or real life, answer the following questions in a class or group discussion:
- Why are gangs formed?
- Why do people choose to belong to gangs?
- How do gangs express themselves?
- What are gang rivalries based upon?

Drama Improvisation

Improvise the scenes in *Ruckus* that happen out of sight of the audience. What really happens when the two schools meet? How violent is it?

Writing

Design a manifesto for either the St Nectan's or the Riverdale Comprehensive gang. You might include details or drawings of how they would wear their school uniform to signify their allegiance. Try to think about how or why pupils choose to identify with their school.

SHAKESPEAREAN LANGUAGE

David Farr borrows many of his characters' predicaments from Shakespearean comedy. Tamsen's and Cath's identity swap, and the confusion that ensues from it, may well remind the audience of the events that unfold in Shakespeare's play, *A Midsummer Night's Dream*. In that play, four young lovers wandering the Athenian woods one midsummer night are subjected to the magical meddling of Puck, an other-worldly sprite who bears a strong resemblance to the character of Cupid in *Ruckus in the Garden*.

You can see from the following extracts how David Farr deliberately echoes *A Midsummer Night's Dream* in his play. Tamsen, in trying to persuade Hugh that she isn't really Cath, uses the same imagery as Shakespeare's Helena does in declaring her unrequited love for Demetrius:

Ruckus in the Garden

Enter **Hugh** *followed by* **Tamsen**.

HUGH	Will you please get your friend off my back.
TAMSEN	I am Tamsen! I'm not letting you go.
BILLIE	Cath?
TAMSEN	I'm not Cath!
BILLIE	Oh God she's really lost it.
TAMSEN	I love you Hugh. You can do what you want with me. Beat me, use me as your spaniel, I am not letting go!

Page 60

87

A Midsummer Night's Dream

> **HELENA**   I am your spaniel; and, Demetrius,
> The more you beat me, I will fawn on you.
> Use me but as your spaniel, spurn me, strike me,
> Neglect me, lose me; only give me leave,
> Unworthy as I am, to follow you.
> What worser place can I beg in your love,
> And yet a place of high respect with me,
> Than to be used as you use your dog?
>
> Act Two, Scene One, lines 203–210.

Discussion

- What similarities can you find between the words of Tamsen and Helena?

- What is the effect of this knowing echo of Shakespeare's text here? Is it humorous, poetic or ironic? Does it create bathos or do you think it is intended to elevate Tamsen's character?

Irony: Figure of speech in which the intended meaning is the opposite of that expressed by the words used.

Bathos: Comical descent from the elevated to the everyday in writing or speech; an anticlimax.

Now look at the next two speeches. The first is spoken by Puck in *A Midsummer Night's Dream*, the second by Cupid in *Ruckus in the Garden*. They both occur at the end of each play where, as in the convention of Shakespearean comedy, order is restored once more:

> **PUCK**   If we shadows have offended,
> Think but this, and all is mended,
> That you have but slumber'd here
> While these visions did appear.

And this weak and idle theme,
No more yielding but a dream,
Gentles, do not reprehend:
if you pardon, we will mend:
And, as I am an honest Puck,
If we have unearned luck
Now to 'scape the serpent's tongue,
We will make amends ere long;
Else the Puck a liar call;
So, good night unto you all.
Give me your hands, if we be friends,
And Robin shall restore amends.

Act Five, Scene One, lines 411–427

CUPID Lovers join hands.
Time to exit the gate
And head for the carriages
That solemnly wait.
The journey is long
There is much to discuss
So get out of the garden
And head for the bus!

Page 69

Comparing Texts

- What is the function of the speaker in each case?

- How do they achieve the same effect of sending the audience away in a buoyant mood? Consider the importance of rhythm and rhyme in creating this effect.

- What similarities and difference can you find between the two speeches? What kind of language does each speaker use?

- Again, what do you think is the effect of this Shakespearean echo in a contemporary setting?

CLASSICAL REFERENCES

> TAMSEN Look at this temple. Look at the carvings. They're all kissing, making love. They don't think about what their parents will think!

It's not only Shakespeare's plays that provide a backdrop to *Ruckus in the Garden*. David Farr also gives an important role to the statues of classical gods who watch over the garden. These statues influence the mortals to such an extent that they are almost a second cast of characters in the play. When rehearsing or studying *Ruckus in the Garden* it is worth finding out about who these classical figures are to gain a richer understanding of the play.

Apollo

Apollo is one of the best-known Greek Gods.

Famously handsome and an expert archer, Apollo was the son of Zeus.

Headstrong at first he grew to represent music, poetry, medicine and the civilized arts. He is also known as the Sun God, as according to legend he drove the fiery chariot that was the sun across the sky each day.

His name was borrowed for the American space programme that led to the first moon landing.

Aphrodite/Venus

Aphrodite is the Greek goddess of sexual love and beauty. She was the daughter of Zeus but had many mortal lovers. Venus is her Roman counterpart.

Venus is the Roman Goddess of gardens. She was the mother of Cupid. In classical mythology she became famous for her romantic intrigues, and she is associated with many aspects of femininity.

Flora

Flora is the Roman Goddess of flowers. There is a painting of her on the left. Her name now exists in the well known company, Interflora, who specialize in delivering flowers for special occasions.

> ### Discussion
>
> The names of other characters from Greek and Roman mythology are also associated with 21st century commercial enterprises. See how many you can think of. You may find that they are the names of shops, finance industries or services.

Creative Writing: Venus's Call

In the final scene, Cupid explains that Venus had called and asked him to switch Tam's and Cath's identities so that the two groups would be forced into a calamity which would lead to the reconciliation of their differences.

Imagine what form this call could take. Would it be a formal declaration from the heavens? Or would it have the casual tone of a call on a mobile telephone?

Use the knowledge you have about all the characters and the two schools to write Venus's call to Cupid.

Try and make your speech fit with the style of the rest of the play. Have a look at the speech from *A Midsummer Night's Dream* below. In it the fairy king, Oberon, gives a similar instruction to Puck. How could you draw on his images in your speech? Can you create the same comic effect that David Farr achieves in translating Shakespearean ideas into a contemporary idiom and setting?

OBERON *(to **Puck**)*
> That very time I saw, but thou couldst not,
> Flying between the cold moon and the earth,
> Cupid all arm'd: a certain aim he took
> At a fair vestal throned by the west,
> And loosed his love-shaft smartly from his bow,
> As it should pierce a hundred thousand hearts;
> But I might see young Cupid's fiery shaft
> Quench'd in the chaste beams of the watery moon,
> And the imperial votaress passed on,
> In maiden meditation, fancy-free.
> Yet mark'd I where the bolt of Cupid fell:
> It fell upon a little western flower,
> Before milk-white, now purple with love's wound,
> And maidens call it love-in-idleness.
> Fetch me that flower; the herb I shew'd thee once:
> The juice of it on sleeping eye-lids laid
> Will make or man or woman madly dote
> Upon the next live creature that it sees.
> Fetch me this herb; and be thou here again
> Ere the leviathan can swim a league.
>
> [Act Two, Scene One, lines 154–174]

ADAPTATIONS

David Farr is not the only writer to transpose a classic story to the present day. Theatre directors frequently set productions of Renaissance dramas in the contemporary world. Novelist Daphne Du Maurier reworked the story of *Jane Eyre* in her book, *Rebecca*, mirroring exactly the tale of a young orphaned woman who leaves a life in service to marry a rich, older man with a troubled and mysterious past. Often such transpositions suggest surprising parallels between our world and that of the original text. The recent film, *Clueless*, was particularly successful in translating the class-bound courting rituals of Jane Austen's society into the rigid social heirarchies of an American high school.

Other examples include *Ten things I hate about you*, a version of Shakespeare's *Taming of the Shrew*; *Bridget Jones's Diary*, a knowing tribute to Jane Austen's *Pride and Prejudice*; and *O Brother Where Art Thou*, whose tale of errant cowboys is loosely based on Homer's epic, *The Odyssey*.

What examples can you think of?

Writing

You are a film director pitching a modern version of a classic story to your financial backers. (Ideas for stories to use might include: *Little Women*, *Robin Hood*, *Beauty and the Beast*, or *Red Riding Hood*). Produce a convincing synopsis of the film detailing how you would transpose the plot and characters to a modern scenario.

Presentation

Now present this pitch to other members of the class who will act as your potential backers. They will interrogate you about your intentions and why they should support your project. Have some answers ready to explain why your chosen story is relevant to today.

BODY SWAP

From *Freaky Friday* to *A Winter's Tale*, body swaps have proved a popular subject for film, drama and fiction. They provide an occasion for comedy, but also give us a serious insight into our own and other people's lives. These transformations often involve radical shifts in class, age or gender: from disguising yourself as a male servant to be close to the man you love, as Viola does in *Twelfth Night*, to being turned from an undignified donkey to a stallion as in Donkey is in *Shrek 2*.

In *Ruckus in the Garden*, when Tamsen and Cath swap identities they do not undergo an inner change, it is only their outward appearances that alter. The girls remain conscious of who they are, and quickly discover the advantages and disadvantages of their new look.

Cath and Tamsen suffer in different ways from low self-esteem. Cath lacks the confidence to make an impression on the boy she really likes. Tamsen distrusts the boys who like her, suspecting they are only after one thing. The body swap experience allows both of them to overcome their insecurities and to realize that beauty is not defined by externals alone.

Discussion

What pressures are there to look a certain way and where do they come from? Which do you think are the strongest of these influences? How do the cosmetics and fashion industries capitalize on people's insecurities about the way they look?

Writing

You can body swap with anyone for a day. Who will it be and why? Write a description of this experience. What will your day be like? How will other people treat you? Do you prefer it to your ordinary life?

PACIFISM

Stanley is a pacifist. He does all he can to stop the ruckus. He feels it is his mission to reconcile the differences between the two schools.

> Pacifist: Someone who believes that violence of any kind is unjustifiable and that one should not participate in war.

Research

Find out about famous pacifists of the twentieth century such as Martin Luther King, Mahatma Gandhi, Nelson Mandela, or the conscientious objectors to World War One and Two. What did they believe in and what methods did they use to try to achieve their goals?

CREATIVE PARTNERSHIPS

The schools are embarked upon a Creative Partnerships project. 'Creative Partnerships' is a government-sponsored creativity programme. Find out all about the organization at: http://www.creative-partnerships.com/aboutcp/

Once you have researched similar creative partnership projects (look in the geography and art sections) you should create the activity and information pack you think the characters in this play are studying.

Writing

In compiling your own activity pack, you should create as much background information as you can from what you know about the gardens from this period. Set specific tasks for students to do. You may want to base the project on an historical garden near your school. You may even be able to arrange a school visit there to get ideas. Your history teacher may be able to help in giving you some good ideas about this or point you in the direction of books on your local area. Alternatively, you could visit your local tourist information office to ask for information.

Explore the websites of the National Trust and English Heritage to find gardens in your area that you could visit:

www.nationaltrust.org.uk   www.english-heritage.org.uk

Further reading and resources

You'll find the National Trust's website for Stourhead Gardens extremely useful in researching the play's setting:

http://www.nationaltrust.org.uk/main/w-vh/w-visits/w-findaplace/w-stourhead/w-stourhead-garden.htm

You might like to look at some of the other novels mentioned in the play:

George Eliot, *Middlemarch*

Maisy is reading George Eliot's famous novel, first published in 1872. The story of *Middlemarch* is set in Tipton Grange, a fictitious stately home, in the 1830s. The book's heroine Dorothea is an heiress with a social conscience who falls in love with a penniless young radical called Will Ladislaw. She finally marries him against the wishes of her dead husband and the stipulations of his will. George Eliot herself took advantage of an assumed identity, publishing under a man's name rather than her own, which was Mary Ann Evans.

Jane Austen, *Emma* and *Pride and Prejudice*

Jane Austen gets two mentions in the play. The first is when Maisy subconsciously compares Rock to Mr. Knightley, a character in her favourite Austen novel, *Emma*. The second time is more flippant but equally telling, as it reveals something of Hugh's romantic nature, when he reminds Tamsen: 'We went to see *Pride and Prejudice*! We kissed at the same time that the guy from *Spooks* kissed Keira Knightley! I bought you popcorn!'